Really Funny Real Words

MARVIN TERBAN

Superdupers!

Really Funny Real Words

Illustrated by
GIULIO MAESTRO

CLARION BOOKS
NEW YORK

For Ann Troy,
a superduper editor!

Clarion Books
a Houghton Mifflin Company imprint
52 Vanderbilt Avenue, New York, NY 10017
Text copyright © 1989 by Marvin Terban
Illustrations copyright © 1989 by Giulio Maestro

Printed in the USA

Library of Congress Cataloging-in-Publication Data

Terban, Marvin.
Superdupers!: really funny real words / by Marvin Terban;
illustrated by Giulio Maestro.
p.   cm.
Bibliography: p.
Includes index.
Summary: Explains the meaning and origins of over 100 nonsense words that make
the English language more colorful including such examples as "flip-flop," "fuzzy-wuzzy," "cancan," and "tutti-frutti."
ISBN 0-89919-804-X: $12.95. — ISBN 0-395-51123-2 (pbk.): $4.95
1. Vocabulary — Juvenile literature. 2. Play on words — Juvenile literature. 3. English language —
Etymology — Juvenile literature. [1. Vocabulary. 2. Play on words. 3. English language — Etymology.]
I. Maestro, Giulio, ill. II. Title.
PE 1449.T45 1989   88-38325
428.1 — dc19   CIP
                                                                                  AC
HCPPAAL10987654321

Contents

Introduction

Words in English come from many different sources such as ancient languages or people's names. Many other words are just made up. Here are some examples of made-up words. Do you know what this sentence means?

The **roly-poly bigwig pooh-poohed** his **humdrum** life and wanted to go to a **razzle-dazzle wingding.**

It means:

The chubby important person hated his boring life and wanted to go to an exciting party.

All the words in dark print were made up by writers and speakers because they wanted new words to name or describe things. Let's call these words *superdupers*. Some of these words are used every day. You might read others in a book or hear people saying them in old movies.

How were these words formed? Some are rhymes, like **claptrap** (see Chapter 1). Some are near-rhymes, like **riffraff** (see Chapter 2). Other words imitate real sounds, like **clickety-clack** (see Chapter 2). Sometimes a sound is repeated to make a new word, like **boo-boo** (see Chapter 3).

These words add life and fun to English. They're imaginative and vivid, and they help our language to grow in colorful ways. In this book you'll discover over one hundred *superdupers* and you'll find out what they mean.

Word experts don't always agree about where all these words came from, but this book will tell you some of the most interesting origins. We can also imagine how other words were made up.

Now when you read one of these words or hear someone say one, you won't get the **heebie-jeebies**. You'll know the meaning **lickety-split**. And because a language grows when people add to it, you can think up some of your own words too. That will be **superduper**!

·1·

Rhymes

People have always loved the sound of rhymes. Sometimes a person takes a word, adds a rhyming sound, and creates a new word! Sometimes real sounds that people make or hear just rhyme by themselves. Sometimes rhyming words in English come from rhyming words in foreign languages. Whatever their origins, these rhyming *superdupers* have been favorites of speakers and writers for years because they add **razzle-dazzle** to our language and keep it from being **humdrum**. **Okey-dokey**, let's begin.

Two- and Three-Syllable Words That Rhyme

"Bill is a **bigwig** billionaire in the billiards business."

✴ Years ago, men wore wigs. The more important the man, the bigger the wig. So it's easy to see why today we call a person of great authority, position, or influence a bigwig.

"'**Boohoo**,' wailed the baby when she broke her favorite toy."

✴ When people cry loudly, they make a sound like boohoo.

"The dog barked '**bow-wow**' when she spotted the stranger."

✴ Bow-wow imitates the sounds dogs make when they bark.

"Don't believe a word he says. It's all **claptrap**."

✴ Years ago, some performers did flashy stunts to get the audience to applaud. These tricks trapped people into clapping. Clap + trap = claptrap. A new word was born that today means worthless speech that someone uses just to win praise.

"She does such silly things. She's a real **ding-a-ling**."

✳ This sarcastic word means a foolish person who acts weirdly. Once people who did or said peculiar things were thought to hear bells ringing ("ding-a-ling") in their heads.

"She likes to **hobnob** with all the fancy, important people."

✳ Hobnob means to be friends with someone. The word might have come from *habbe* or *nabbe* (meaning "have and have not"), two old English words that became one word and changed meaning.

"The **hobo** raked the leaves, and my mother gave him supper."

✳ A person who wanders from place to place doing odd jobs used to be called a hobo, but this word isn't used much today. It might have come from a sarcastic greeting. "Beau" (pronounced like the bow on a gift) used to mean a person who is concerned about his appearance. Tramps usually don't care how they look. An insulting person might have once called to a tramp, "Hey, beau!" The phrase caught on and got shortened into one rhyming word, "hobo."

"Clean up this horrible **hodgepodge**, Horace!"

✳ A hodgepodge is a mess, a jumble of junk. The word comes from two old French words *hocher* (to shake) and *pot*. Can you see how shaking a big pot full of different things could make a hodgepodge?

"Your majesty, the **hoi polloi** are knocking at the palace gates."

※ Some people high up in society might call the common, ordinary people the hoi polloi. The phrase comes from Greek, and it means "the many."

"What's all the **hubbub**, hippo? I'm trying to sleep."

※ A loud confusion of many sounds is called a hubbub. Some people who study languages think it came from the old Irish word *hooboobbes*, a war cry meaning "Victory!" Soldiers used to shout this word in battle. That must have been very noisy.

"He hated his **humdrum** job and yearned for some excitement."

✴ A hum is a continuous, boring sound that doesn't change. A speaker or writer may once have added "drum" to "hum" to double its sound and intensify its meaning. He thereby created a new word that means dull, monotonous, tedious, and lacking variety. How boring!

"Now Ken's cow won't **kowtow** to Karen's cat."

✴ Years ago in China, if a person wanted to show deep respect or submission to another person, he would kneel and touch his forehead to the ground. That greeting was called a kowtow. Today when someone kowtows to another person, he's fawning and flattering and obeying like a slave in order to seek favor or attention.

"Don't call me a **nitwit**! I have more brains than you!"

✳ Nitwit is an insulting slang word for a stupid or silly person. It might have come from *nichts* (German for "nothing"), plus "wit" ("intelligence"). Someone might have rudely called another person a nitwit to suggest that he had nothing for intelligence.

"I may be a **peewee** now, but someday I'll grow taller than you!"

✳ Wee means tiny. Once someone might have playfully added "pee" to "wee" to form a new, fun word that means an unusually small person or thing.

"When the bell rang, the children rushed **pell-mell** out of school."

✳ Things in a confused, disorderly manner are pell-mell. This word may come from two old French rhyming words, *pesle mesle*, (meaning "to mix things up").

"They're having a perfectly pleasant **powwow**."

✹ Here's an Algonquian Indian word for a conference or meeting, but it's used in English all the time.

"You can't go out with him. He's one of the **ragtag** mob."

✹ "Rag" and "tag" both mean a dirty, torn piece of cloth. Perhaps someone once wanted a new word to name people he thought were crude and not respectable. Since they usually wore tattered, filthy clothing, he called them ragtag.

"Don't trust him. He's full of **razzmatazz**."

✹ This slang word for something flashy that's meant to dazzle or trick you is another way to say "razzle-dazzle" (see page 30).

"**Rinky-dink** things usually fall apart fast."

✳ Anything that is inferior or tasteless can be called rinky-dink. This word probably came from the slang word "dinky," meaning small or insignificant. Maybe someone once just rhymed "dinky" with "rinky" to suggest something extremely cheap or gaudy.

"We had a wild and wonderful **wingding** on New Year's eve."

✳ Wingding means a lively, lavish party that is sometimes very noisy, but nobody knows exactly where this word originated. What do you think?

Superduper Snapshots

A Humdrum Powwow.

A Peewee Ding-a-Ling
Speaking Claptrap.

The Hubbub of the Ragtag Hoi Polloi.

The Hodgepodge after the Wingding.

"Boohoo!" and "Bow-wow!"

Four- (and More)-Syllable Words That Rhyme

"I love to hear him play **boogie-woogie**."

✹ This is a style of playing fast jazz on the piano. There are eight beats to the measure and a repeated pattern in the bass.

"When you pay me what you owe me, we'll be **even-steven**."

✹ One of the many meanings of "even" is that you don't owe me anything and I don't own you anything. We're even. How "steven" got into this phrase more than one hundred years ago is anyone's guess, probably just because it rhymes with even. By the way, you'll sometimes see even-steven written three other ways: even-Steven, even-stephen, and even-Stephen. Steve gets around, doesn't he?

"She's such a **fuddy-duddy**. She doesn't like any of the new styles."

✳ Nobody is quite sure where this word comes from. But "fuddy" sounds a little like "fussy," and "dud" means a failure, something that doesn't work right. That might explain why a fuddy-duddy is a person who is old-fashioned, unimaginative, and fussy. He or she is sometimes called an "old fogy."

"He loves his new stuffed panda. It's so **fuzzy-wuzzy**."

✳ A fuzz is a mass of light, fine fibers like soft hair or fur. (It might have come from a German word, *fussig*, meaning spongy.) Anything that's fuzzy-wuzzy is more than just fuzzy.

"Hannah has a **handy-dandy** candy fanner."

✳ If something is easy to handle and is a dandy, practical object to use, then handy-dandy is a perfect way to describe it.

I like my candies cool!

YUMMY RED HOTS

"While I'm out of the room, I want none of your **hanky-panky**!"

✴ Any tricky or mischievous activity can be called hanky-panky. A magician sometimes uses a handkerchief ("hanky") in a trick to fool the audience's eyes. Hanky-panky can fool you too.

"When the lions got loose, the clowns raced **harum-scarum** for the exit."

✴ This word describes actions that are rash, hasty, and done with no sense of responsibility. Imagine a hare (an animal that looks like a big rabbit) who is scared. What would it do? It would probably run around wildly and recklessly. Some people think harum-scarum might have come from "hare" plus "scare."

"I get the **heebie-jeebies** every time I pass this scary old house."

✳ Years ago a cartoonist named Billy DeBeck made up this phrase for his comic strip called "Barney Google." He wanted a new way of saying a nervous or jumpy feeling (sometimes called "the willies" or "the jitters").

"The gorilla opened the cages, and the animals ran **helter-skelter** around the zoo."

✳ This word means in a hurried, confused, disorderly, hasty, careless manner just like "harum-scarum." Nobody seems to know where it came from. What do you think?

23

"Close that window! Everything's blowing **higgledy-piggledy** in here!"

✴Anything in utter disorder or confusion is higgledy-piggledy. Some people think that this word came from "pig." Pigs do make a mess, don't they? "Pig" grew to "piggle," and then to "piggledy." Then, to make the word funnier, someone added "higgledy" at the front.

"The magician performed a bit of **hocus-pocus** when she made the elephant appear in the thimble."

✴A magician sometimes says, "Hocus-pocus!" (words that don't mean anything) when doing hocus-pocus (tricks that deceive your eyes).

"I don't like him so much because he always acts so **hoity-toity**."

✳ A snobby, snooty, stuck-up person behaves in a hoity-toity way. It used to be "highty-tighty," maybe from "high" (meaning superior) because someone felt higher or better than someone else.

It is utterly beneath me to descend to your level!

"Line up, folks, and we'll dance the **hokeypokey** and the **hully-gully**."

✳ At different times hokeypokey has meant a cheat or swindle, any cheap thing, and ice cream sold on the street. How did one word get to have all these different meanings? Some people think they might have come from "hocus-pocus." But how? What's your guess? Now many people think of the hokeypokey and the hully-gully as simple group dances.

"'**Holy moly**!' he cried when he saw his birthday present."

✴ There are several exclamations of surprise and wonder that begin with "holy" like "Holy cow!" and "Holy mackerel!" and "Holy smoke!" It's not clear why cow and mackerel and smoke are used, but the only one that rhymes is "Holy moly!"

"Everything's just **hotsy-totsy** now that you're here."

✴ This word (meaning satisfactory, pleasing, fine) was especially popular in the 1920s, but you still might hear it today. If you were shivering in the cold, you'd probably wish things were hotsy-totsy again.

"'Listen to that **hurdy-gurdy**, Gertie,' said Bertie."

✴ A hurdy-gurdy is a musical instrument like a hand or barrel organ. It is usually played on the street by a musician (called an organ-grinder) who turns a crank or handle. He tries to attract crowds and collect money.

"When the home team lost the big game, there was plenty of **hurly-burly** in the stands."

✳ Years ago the word "hurling" meant a disorderly commotion or noisy disturbance. Hurly-burly means the same thing today and is just a rhyming form of that old word.

"Can you believe that fat cat was once an **itty-bitty** kitty?"

✳ A bit is a small piece of something. So it's easy to see how something very tiny could be called itty-bitty (or sometimes itsy-bitsy).

"**Jeepers creepers**! Look at all those peepers!"

✳ Someone might cry out this phrase to express great surprise or dismay.

"They're such a **lovey-dovey** couple."

✸A dove is a bird associated with love and peace. A lovey-dovey person is gentle and very affectionate.

"The chef will perform a little **mumbo jumbo** in the kitchen and turn all these leftovers into a fabulous feast."

✸In Mandingo, an African language, the word *mā-mā-gyo-mbō* meant a magician who could make the troubled spirits of a person's ancestors go away. Today mumbo jumbo can mean any confusing rituals, magic words, or amazing actions.

"Don't be so **namby-pamby**. Get in there and feed that lion!"

✳ Anyone who is weak, cowardly, or unable to make a decision could rudely be called namby-pamby. The word came from a man's name. Ambrose Philips wrote emotional poems about country life in the 1700s. Another writer wanted to make mean fun of the poems, so he took Ambrose's nickname, Namby, and made up an insulting word, namby-pamby.

"Now we're getting down to the **nitty-gritty** of the crime."

✳ The hard core of a matter, the harsh truth, the practical details, and the most basic elements all can be called the nitty-gritty. That's because "grit' means very small, hard particles of sand or stone. If you're searching for something and you're examining tiny bits of things, you're really getting to the nitty-gritty, aren't you?

"**Okey-dokey** class, you can have the rest of the day off."

✳ The first two letters in okey-dokey (or okie-dokie) are OK. That's how the word got started, and that's why it means satisfactory, all right, agreeable, and fine. OK?

"Penny's getting pretty **palsy-walsy** with Pauline."

✳ A pal is a buddy or friend. Someone wanted to make up a word that meant really friendly and chummy, so he coined palsy-walsy. He could also have said "buddy-buddy" (see page 50).

"I love all the **razzle-dazzle** at the circus."

✳ "Dazzle" means spectacular brightness, so anything that's razzle-dazzle is showy, exciting, and brilliant.

30

"Isn't this **roly-poly** pig adorable?"

✴ Short and plump people or animals are called roly-poly. Maybe that's because "roll" means to move along like a ball. The imaginative person who made up this word might have thought that a pudgy little person or animal moved like a ball.

"It was a **rootin'-tootin'** day at the ball field."

✴ When you root for your favorite team or toot a horn, you make loud noises. So anything that's rootin'-tootin' is noisy, cheerful, exciting, and enthusiastic.

"That was a **superduper** party, wasn't it?"

✴ Superduper is a great, marvelous, and terrific word because it means great, marvelous, and terrific. It also means excellent, ideal, and first-rate! "Super" refers to something that's superior or better than something else. So anything that's more super than super must be superduper!

31

"Cut me just a **teeny-weeny** slice of pie, Tina. I'm on a diet."

✳ "Teeny" is another way of saying tiny and "wee" means tiny. Teeny-weeny (or teensy-weensy) is a rhyming form of teeny that means very, extremely, extraordinarily small.

"Twenty-two scoops of **tutti-frutti** ice cream, please."

✳ In Italian, *tutti-frutti* means "all fruits." In English, the word has much the same meaning. It describes food that tastes like many fruit flavors together.

"She's the biggest **wheeler-dealer** in the business."

✳ One of the slang definitions of "wheel" is to do things to make yourself richer or more important. So a wheeler-dealer tries to make lots of business deals to get money and power for himself or herself.

"Will you marry Milly or won't you, Willy? Don't be a **willy-nilly**."

✳ This comes from a very old expression, "Will I, nill I?" that means "Am I willing (to do something) or am I unwilling?" Today it can mean that you can't make up your mind and don't know what to do next (as in the sentence above). It can also mean that something will happen whether you want it to or not, with or against your wishes, as in: "There's nothing you can do about it, Billy. Willy will marry Milly, willy-nilly.

By the way, did you notice how many of these colorful words mean in a wild confusion or a jumbled mess?

harum-scarum, **helter-skelter**,
higgledy-piggledy, **hodgepodge**, **hurly-burly**,
and **pell-mell**

But now you won't ever be confused by this mess of words.

More Superduper Snapshots

A Hoity-Toity Namby-Pamby Fuddy-Duddy

A Roly-Poly Playing the Boogie-Woogie

An Itsy-Bitsy, Teensy-Weensy Hurdy-Gurdy

Holy Moly! Jeepers Creepers!

A Higgledy-Piggledy Hurly-Burly

A Rootin'-Tootin' Wheeler-Dealer Dancing the Hokeypokey

·2·

Almost-Rhymes

To be a fun *superduper*, a word doesn't have to rhyme exactly. Sometimes it can almost rhyme.

Two-Syllable Almost-Rhymes

"Chiquita and Chad had a **chitchat** about Chuck's chimp's chances for the championship."

✳ An old English word, *chatteren*, was supposed to sound like people talking and talking. From that word came our words "chatter," "chat," and the almost-rhyming word chitchat, which means light conversation, small talk, and gossip.

"**Dingdong**! The ice cream man is here."

✳ The word imitates the real sound of a bell ringing.

"And what do you do with this **doodad**, dad?"

✳ Any gadget whose name you can't think of can be called a doodad (or sometimes a "doohickey"). Can you think of why?

I'm afraid that it's just a worthless doohickey.

DOODADS FOR SALE

YOU NEED THEM!
YOU WANT THEM!

"You mean to tell me that Phyllis fell for that foolish **flimflam**?"

✳ *Flim,* an old Norse word, meant mockery, and today flimflam means any kind of tricky nonsense, deception, swindle, or fraud. Watch out for it!

"First he was for it. Then he was against it. He certainly does **flip-flop**, doesn't he?"

★ This word can mean a backward somersault or handspring, but today it often refers to a complete change of direction or action. Originally people thought the word sounded like repeated flapping.

"When the donkey saw the farmer fall into the mud, he began to **hee-haw** noisily."

★ The word sounds exactly like the braying of a donkey. When a person laughs loudly, he sometimes sounds like a donkey, doesn't he?

"When I asked her what she thought of my invention, all she could say was, '**Ho-hum**.' "

★ The word sounds just like a yawn, and that's why it expresses boredom.

"Don't touch a single **knickknack** on those shelves."

✳ "Knack" can mean an object, a thing. Knickknack expands that word to mean a small, fancy, decorative ornament on display. A knickknack is also a piece of *bric-à-brac*, a French word for a collection of small objects displayed for their beauty, rarity, or age.

"For dinner, we're having a **mishmash** of whatever's in the refrigerator."

✳ A mishmash is a hodgepodge (see page 12), a collection of unrelated objects. "Mash" is a mixture of things, usually feed for cows. When lots of things are mixed together, it's a mishmash.

"Penelope Putnam is the popular **Ping-Pong** personality of Punxsutawney, Pennsylvania."

💥 To the person who made up this word (as a brand name for table tennis equipment), the bouncing ball made a sound like "ping pong."

"You're too good for him, my dear. He's just one of the **riffraff**."

💥 Crude people with bad reputations are sometimes called the riffraff. This word came from two old English words, *rif* and *raf*, meaning "one and all."

"Did you see what I saw, a giant **seesaw**?"

💥 In a playground you'll find a seesaw, a long piece of wood balanced in the middle. If two people sit on the ends of the plank, one can ride up while the other rides down. When you saw a piece of wood, your arm moves up and down. Now you see how seesaw comes from "saw."

And you should see the monsters that ride on it!

"The baby loved to **splish-splash** in the tub."

✳ The splish-splash of water is much more than just the splash or dash or swish of it. It's the splish-splash of it.

"Never tell Tilly a tale because Tilly is a terrible **telltale**."

✳ A person who reveals secrets about other people is a telltale because he or she tells tales.

"I was trying to sleep, but the **ticktock** of the clock kept me awake."

✳ Doesn't "ticktock" sound exactly like the sound of an old-fashioned clock?

"The athlete was in **tip-top** shape from the tip of her toes to the top of her head."

✷ Tip is the end; top is the highest point. What could be higher (or better or more excellent) than the end of the highest point, the tip of the top?

"We saw the bolts of lightning **zigzag** across the night sky."

✷ When you zigzag you move from side to side with short, sharp turns. Zigzag came from the German word *zickzack*, which came from *zacke*, which means point or tooth. Pointed teeth do zigzag, don't they. And the letter *z* itself is a zigzaggy letter.

There he goes shooting off at the mouth again!

Four-Syllable Almost-Rhymes

"Don't **dilly-dally**. The submarine's leaving!"

✸ "Dally" comes from the old French word *dalier*, meaning to waste time, dawdle, loiter, or linger. Dilly-dally is a more fun way of saying just plain dally and adds colorful emphasis.

" 'Oh, **fiddle-faddle**!' cried Phyllis. 'I forgot where I parked the camel again.' "

✸ "Fiddle" can mean nonsense and stupidity. When someone is getting annoyed or impatient about something, it's natural she would want to say more than just "fiddle," so she says "fiddle-faddle!"

"Don't worry. Everything's **hunky-dory** now."

✳This word came from old Dutch words and has been common in English for at least a hundred years. It means perfectly all right, quite satisfactory, and just fine.

"Jack and Jill went up the hill to **jibber-jabber**."

✳When someone jabbers, he talks rapidly. His words are often meaningless. "Jabber" comes from an old English word, *jaberen*, which sort of sounds like fast speech that's difficult to understand. When you jibber-jabber, you really talk nonsense.

"Her bracelets went **jingle-jangle** as she danced wildly."

✳ "Jingle" and "jangle" are the ringing sounds that pieces of metal make when they touch each other lightly. They come from *ginglen* and *janglen*, two old English words. When you put "jingle" and "jangle" together, they sound like tinkling and clinking, don't they?

"I love to hear the **pitter-patter** of little feet on the stairs."

✳ The word is supposed to sound just like a rapid series of light tapping sounds such as rain beating on a rooftop or footsteps of little children.

"This time don't **shilly-shally**. Start your homework immediately."

✳ This word came from the expression "Shill I? or shall I?" spoken years ago by a person who couldn't make up his or her mind. That's why today shilly-shally means to hesitate, waver, or delay.

"After the big frog hopped wildly around the room, everything was **topsy-turvy**."

✳ When the top is down and the bottom is up and everything is in a state of complete disorder and confusion, that's topsy-turvy. The word "topsy" comes from "top," of course. *Tervy* is an obsolete English word meaning "to turn."

"How dare you talk to me like that, you little **whippersnapper**!"

✳Whippersnapper means a rude, insignificant person. The word came from "snippersnapper," which might have come from "snippet" (which can mean a small or mischievous person) or "snippy" (which means rude). What do you think?

"I need a decision today. Make up your mind. Don't be so **wishy-washy**."

✳Water is thin and loose, not strong or firm. A weak-willed person who can't make up his or her mind is like water that you wash with — wishy-washy.

Come on, let's be partners!

47

Here's a little animal story for you made up of more four-syllable *superdupers:*

When the animals heard the train go by **clickety-clack**, they all rushed **lickety-split** to meet the farmer at the station. The horse trotted **clippety-clop**, the rabbit ran **hippety-hop**, the frog leaped **flippety-flop**, and the turkey talked **gobbledygook**.

As we've seen before, many of the words in this book are meant to imitate real sounds. Five of the six words on this page do just that. The sound of a train on tracks does sound like "clickety-clack." When a horse trots, its hooves do make a "clippety-clop" sound. "Hippety-hop" and "flippety-flop" are words that imitate the sounds some animals (or even people) can make when they move. "Gobbledygook" means wordy talk that's unclear. It comes from "gobble," the sound a turkey makes, plus "gook," which means a dirty or sludgy substance. By the way, anybody can talk gobbledygook, not just a turkey. "Lickety-split" means very fast because one of the meanings of "lick" is to move quickly and rapidly.

·3·

Supersuper Duperdupers Words That Double Up

To make up a fun word, you don't have to rhyme or nearly rhyme sounds. You can just repeat them. Doubling the sounds adds to the meaning and makes the word more expressive.

"Bonita bought a **bonbon**."

✳ This is a candy with fruit, nuts, or creamy sugar paste in the middle and chocolate or sugar paste all around. In French, *bon* means good. Many people think this candy is doubly good (*bonbon*).

They're yum-yum!

BONBONS
sweet as nectar!

"The baboon has a **boo-boo** on his belly."

✳This comes from "boohoo" (see page 10) because when someone gets a boo-boo (an injury) they often cry, "Boohoo!" It can also mean a stupid, thoughtless mistake that can injure someone's feelings and make him or her cry.

"Buster and Bud are **buddy-buddy**."

✳A "buddy" is a friend, a pal. When you double the word you strengthen the meaning to mean really friendly.

"Can you **cancan**?"

✳ The cancan is a lively, high-kicking dance from France. The French word for duck is *canard*. A duck walks with high, waddling movements a little like the steps in the dance.

"Watch Charlie's chicken **cha-cha**."

✳ This is an American Spanish word for a ballroom dance that came from Latin America. You dance it with lots of rhythm.

"I can't stand them. They're so **goody-goody**."

✳ Again, by doubling a word like good, a writer or speaker can intensify its meaning. Goody-goody means much more than just plain good. It means extremely sweet or extraordinarily good, often in a phony way.

" '**Ha-ha**!' laughed the police officer. 'Now I've got you!' "

✳ Laughing sounds like "ha-ha." Sometimes people put stronger emphasis on the second "ha," like this: ha-HA! That sometimes means "I've caught you!" or "I've got it!"

"And these are our **huggy-huggy** hippos."

✳ If you hug someone, you're being affectionate. If you're huggy-huggy, you're being extremely affectionate and "lovey-dovey" (see page 28).

"We must keep this news strictly **hush-hush**."

✳ Hush-hush comes from an old English word, *huissht*, which describes anything really quiet, secret, or confidential. When you absolutely, positively don't want anyone in the whole world to know your secret, keep it hush-hush.

"Don't do that, Norbert. That's a **no-no**."

✴ "No" is a negative word. It's the opposite of "yes." It's the word you say when you can't or won't do something. You use it to disagree with someone, or to deny or refuse something. Therefore, a no-no is definitely anything that's wrong or that you shouldn't do.

"Penny, shake that **pom-pom**!"

✴ Pom-pom comes from the French word *pompon*, which means a small, round flower. Today a pom-pom is also a ball of material such as wool used to decorate a cap, or paper streamers on a stick. Cheerleaders or sports fans often wave pom-poms at a ball game to cheer on the home team.

"Poor Peter! The president **pooh-poohed** his plans."

✴ Pooh-pooh is the double of "pooh," a word used to express dislike, scorn, or contempt. Maybe somebody once saw something he or she didn't like and wanted to make light of. The person said, "Pooh!" as if spitting at it. The word caught on and doubled.

"Ray is so **rah-rah** about everything at school."

✳ Someone (perhaps in the 1920s) took the second half of "hurrah" (a shout of joy, victory, or praise) and doubled it to make "rah-rah." This new, short, expressive word describes people who are spirited and enthusiastic about things like sporting events or social activities.

"Sonia sang the solo with a **so-so** voice."

✳ Maybe somebody in describing something once said or wrote that it wasn't so good and it wasn't so bad. It was just so-so, just average.

"Tim took Tom's **tom-tom**."

✳ In Hindi (a language of northern India), a tamtam is a small-headed drum, usually long and narrow, that is beaten with the hands. The word imitates the sound of the drum. "Tom-tom" is our version of the word tamtam.

54

"Trudy tromped on Tallulah's **tutu**."

 *Tutu* is a French word for a very short ballet skirt with many layers of gathered, sheer fabric.

"Yolanda is a young **yo-yo** champion."

 To make a yo-yo you need a flat spool, a string, and a finger. Wrap the string around the spool and tie one end to your finger. Spin the spool up and down by moving your finger and hand. Yo-yo was originally the brand name of the company that made this toy. Today everybody calls a yo-yo a yo-yo regardless of who manufactures it.

"**Yum-yum**, mom. This plum is wonderful!"

 "Yum" sounds a little like the sound your lips might make when you're chewing delightfully delicious food. Try it and see.

Munch, munch.

What's My Name?

A play in one act

Imagine you're on a television game show called "What's My Name?" Mystery guests appear on stage, but you can't see them. You're blindfolded. You have to guess their names. All you know is that each mystery guest has a double name like the words in Chapter 3 of this book. All you can say to each guest is, "How do you feel?" From their answers, you have to guess their names. You can act out the script below with your friends, or you can use it as an example of how to make up your own quiz show following the rules above.

HOST:　　　　　　And now it's time to play "What's My Name?" And here's our first mystery guest.

YOU:	How do you feel?
BONBON:	I feel sugary sweet.
YOU:	Your name is Bonbon.
HOST:	You're right! And here is guest number two.
YOU:	How do you feel?
BUDDY-BUDDY:	I feel that you're a real pal to ask.
YOU:	That must be Buddy-buddy.
HOST:	Right again! Mystery guest number three, please enter.
YOU:	How do you feel?
BOO-BOO:	I feel injured because I hurt my knee.
YOU:	That could be nobody else but Boo-boo.
HOST:	You're on your way to the championship. Here's number four.
YOU:	How do you feel?
CANCAN:	I feel like kicking up my legs!
YOU:	Cancan, is that you?
HOST:	It sure is! Now here's guest number five.
YOU:	How do you feel?
CHA-CHA:	I feel rhythmic.
YOU:	It's Cha-cha, I think.
HOST:	You think right. Now try number six.
YOU:	How do you feel?
GOODY-GOODY:	I feel that's too, too nice of you to inquire.

YOU:	That sounds like Goody-goody.
HOST:	Good! Can you guess the name of number seven?
YOU:	How do you feel?
HA-HA:	I feel in a funny mood.
YOU:	Only Ha-ha could be in a funny mood.
HOST:	It's Ha-ha, all right. Now here's number eight.
YOU:	How do you feel?
HUGGY-HUGGY:	I feel affectionate.
YOU:	I'll give you a hug later, Huggy-huggy.
HOST:	Number nine, please step center stage.
YOU:	How do you feel?
HUSH-HUSH:	I feel that it's a secret how I feel.
YOU:	I won't tell your secret, Hush-hush.
HOST:	Can you tell who number ten is?
YOU:	How do you feel?
NO-NO:	I feel that's a question I shouldn't answer.
YOU:	You think it's a no-no, No-no?
HOST:	Oh, no! You're right! Number eleven, step up, please.
YOU:	How do you feel?
POOH-POOH:	I feel that's a dumb question.
YOU:	Why do you pooh-pooh the question, Pooh-pooh?
HOST:	Just a few more and you're the champ. Number twelve.

YOU:	How do you feel?
POM-POM:	I feel cheer-ful.
YOU:	Pom-pom, I'd know you anywhere!
HOST:	Lucky number thirteen, you're our next mystery guest.
YOU:	How do you feel?
RAH-RAH:	I feel terrific! Great! Sensational!
YOU:	So do I, Rah-rah.
HOST:	Number fourteen, get ready to answer.
YOU:	How do you feel?
SO-SO:	I feel all right. Not too bad. Not too good.
YOU:	Just so-so, eh, So-so?
HOST:	We're nearing the end. Here's guest number fifteen.
YOU:	How do you feel?
TOM-TOM:	I feel the beat.
YOU:	Then you must be Tom-tom.
HOST:	Right you are. Now, number sixteen.
YOU:	How do you feel?
TUTU:	I feel like spinning on my toes.
YOU:	Me too, Tutu.
HOST:	The last two. Here's number seventeen.
YOU:	How do you feel?
YUM-YUM:	I feel delicious.
YOU:	That makes me hungry, Yum-yum.
HOST:	And now our final guest, number eighteen.

YOU:	How do you feel?
YO-YO:	I feel that life has its ups and downs.
YOU:	Ups and downs? Ups and downs?
HOST:	Guess this one and you're our new champion.
YOU:	Ups and downs? It must be Yo-yo.
HOST:	Yo-yo it is! Congratulations, You. You are our new national "What's My Name?" champion. By the way, You. What's your name?

Alphabetical Listing of
the Words Featured in This Book

ABCDEFGHIJKLM

NOPQRSTUVWXYZ

Bibliography

The American Heritage Dictionary of the English Language. William Morris, ed. Boston: Houghton Mifflin Co., 1981.

Chapman, Robert L. **American Slang.** New York: Harper & Row, 1987.

Collis, Harry. **Colloquial English.** New York: Regents Publishing Company, Inc., 1981.

Freeman, William. **A Concise Dictionary of English Idioms.** Revised and edited by B.A. Phythian, The Writer, Inc. Boston, 1976.

Partridge, Eric. **Smaller Slang Dictionary.** London: Routledge and Kegan Paul, 1984.

Wentworth, Harold and Stuart Berg Flexner. **The Pocket Dictionary of American Slang.** New York: Pocket Books, 1968.

Whitford, Harold C. and Robert J. Dixson. **Handbook of American Idioms and Idiomatic Usage.** New York: Regents Publishing Company, Inc., 1973.